EYEWITNESS TO HISTORY

HELEN KELLER

in her own words

Gareth Stevens
PUBLISHING

By Caroline Kennon

Please visit our website, www.garethstevens.com. For a free color catalog of all our high-quality books, call toll free 1-800-542-2595 or fax 1-877-542-2596.

Library of Congress Cataloging-in-Publication Data

Kennon, Caroline.
Helen Keller in her own words / by Caroline Kennon.
p. cm. — (Eyewitness to history)
Includes index.
ISBN 978-1-4824-1278-9 (pbk.)
ISBN 978-1-4824-0812-6 (6-pack)
ISBN 978-1-4824-1479-0 (library binding)
1. Keller, Helen, — 1880-1968 — Juvenile literature. 2. Sullivan, Annie, — 1866-1936 — Juvenile literature. 3. Deafblind women — United States — Biography — Juvenile literature. I. Title.
HV1624.K4 K46 2015
362.4—d23

First Edition

Published in 2015 by
Gareth Stevens Publishing
111 East 14th Street, Suite 349
New York, NY 10003

Copyright © 2015 Gareth Stevens Publishing

Designer: Katelyn E. Reynolds
Editor: Therese Shea

Photo credits: Cover, pp. 1, 4 (Helen), 9, 11, 15, 16, 17, 19, 21, 27 Library of Congress Prints and Photographs Division; cover, pp. 1 (background image), 25 Imagno/Getty Images; cover, p. 1 (logo quill icon) Seamartini Graphics Media/Shutterstock.com; cover, p. 1 (logo stamp) YasnaTen/Shutterstock.com; cover, p. 1 (color grunge frame) DmitryPrudnichenko/Shutterstock.com; cover, pp. 1–32 (paper background) Nella/Shutterstock.com; cover, pp. 1–32 (decorative elements) Ozerina Anna/Shutterstock.com; pp. 1–32 (wood texture) Reinhold Leitner/Shutterstock.com; pp. 1–32 (open book background) Elena Schweitzer/Shutterstock.com; pp. 1–32 (bookmark) Robert Adrian Hillman/Shutterstock.com; pp. 4–5 (house) Harvey Meston/Archive Photos/Getty Images; p. 7 family member of Thaxter P. Spencer, now part of the R. Stanton Avery Special Collections at the New England Historic Genealogical Society/Wikipedia.com; p. 9 (signature) WikiLaurent/Wikipedia.com; p. 12 alle12/Vetta/Getty Images; p. 13 Topical Press Agency/Getty Images; p. 22 tristan tan/Shutterstock.com; p. 23 Time Life Pictures/Pix Inc./Getty Images; p. 28 RadlovskYaroslav/Shutterstock.com.

Printed in the United States of America

CPSIA compliance information: Batch #CS15GS: For further information contact Gareth Stevens, New York, New York at 1-800-542-2595.

CONTENTS

*Words in the glossary appear in **bold** type the first time they are used in the text.*

The FEVER

Helen Keller was born June 27, 1880, in Tuscumbia, Alabama. She was a healthy baby and very loved. In an **autobiography,** she wrote: *"The beginning of my life was simple and much like every other little life. I came, I saw, I conquered, as the first baby in the family always does."*

When Keller was just 18 months old, she developed a terrible fever: *"They called it **acute congestion** of the stomach and brain. The doctor thought*

Helen Keller

I could not live." When the fever left, the family was overjoyed. However, *"no one, not even the doctor, knew that I should never see or hear again."* Her mother soon learned after the fever faded that her baby had lost her hearing and sight. Helen Keller would be deaf and blind for the rest of her life.

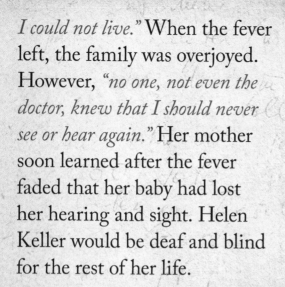

The Keller family home was called Ivy Green.

FIRST WORDS

Helen Keller was a normal baby in every way at first. She began walking when she was about 1. She had already begun saying her first words when she became sick. After she recovered, she remembered the word "water" but, without the practice of hearing adults speak, there was no way for her to improve upon her vocabulary or pronunciation. She said, *"I ceased making the sound 'wah-wah' only when I learned to spell the word."*

ANNE *Sullivan*

BEFORE ANNE

Before Anne Sullivan arrived, Helen Keller had developed her own limited sign language of about 60 signs. She could communicate with the cook's daughter, Martha Washington. They played together, searched for eggs in the yard, and made things in the kitchen. Keller was quite mischievous, though. After she locked her mother in a room for several hours, her parents looked for help. They needed someone to teach Keller how to interact with the world. They needed Anne Sullivan.

Keller's young life was full of struggles. She had to invent ways of asking for things, and miscommunication led to frustration. She often acted out in terrible anger: *"The need of some means of communication became so urgent that . . . outbursts occurred daily."* Keller's parents knew she needed education. However, they *"lived a long way from any school for the blind or the deaf."* The Kellers asked a teacher to come live with them.

When Keller was 6 years old, Anne Sullivan arrived at the Keller home. Sullivan had been nearly blind herself, but a successful operation restored her sight.

She had attended the Perkins School for the Blind in Massachusetts. There, she learned how to communicate with a blind and deaf woman.

Without Anne Sullivan, Helen Keller might never have achieved all that she did. Keller sometimes referred to her in writings, even years later, as "Teacher."

MORE TO KNOW

Anne Sullivan was 20 years old when she accepted a job with the Kellers. Helen Keller described Sullivan's arrival as *"the most important day I remember in all my life."*

7

BREAKTHROUGHS

MORE TO KNOW

Helen Keller struggled at first to understand **abstract** ideas like "loving" and "thinking." Sullivan taught Keller that she couldn't touch love, but she could feel it.

Anne Sullivan used her fingers to spell words on Helen Keller's palm. At first, Keller didn't understand the relationship between the touch of her fingers and objects, but Sullivan **persevered**. Finally, she ran water over Keller's hand and then spelled the word "water." Helen Keller made the connection.

Keller wanted to learn more and quickly. She said, *"From the beginning of my education Miss Sullivan made it a practice to speak to me as she would speak to any hearing child; the only difference was that she spelled the sentences into my hand instead of speaking them."*

Just 4 months after Sullivan arrived, 7-year-old Keller knew how to "finger-spell" hundreds of words and some simple sentences. In 1888, Keller and Sullivan left Alabama so that Keller could attend the Perkins School for the Blind.

Helen Keller put her hands on Anne Sullivan's mouth and throat to understand her without the use of sign language. This was how she learned to read lips.

LEARNING TO WRITE

By 1887, Helen Keller was learning to write. She placed paper over a board that had the alphabet grooved into it. With patience and practice, she memorized how to move her pencil in order to form the letters on her own—and then words, sentences, and finally whole books. She began to write letters to relatives. She sometimes used a ruler to guide her in drawing square block letters.

Helen Keller's actual signature:

Helen Keller

9

In SCHOOL

In 1890, Helen Keller began speech classes at the Horace Mann School for the Deaf in Boston, Massachusetts. Then, beginning in 1894, she attended the Wright-Humason School for the Deaf in New York City

MORE TO KNOW

At Cambridge School, Keller made friends for the first time in her life with girls without her disabilities.

to improve her communication skills and also to study regular academic subjects.

Keller decided to go to college: *"The thought of going to college took root in my heart and became an earnest desire, which **impelled** me to enter into competition for a degree with seeing and hearing girls."*

To prepare, Keller entered the Cambridge School in 1896. Since it wasn't a school for mute or deaf students, Anne Sullivan attended, too: *"Each day Miss Sullivan went to the classes with me and spelled into my hand with infinite patience all that the teachers said."*

"THE FROST KING"

In 1892, Keller wrote a short story called "The Frost King" for the head of the Perkins School for the Blind, who published it. However, it was soon discovered that it was much like another story already published. It was a story Keller had probably read when she was very young. The author of the original work, Margaret Canby, wrote to the upset Keller: *"Some day you will write a great story out of your own head, that will be a comfort and help to many."*

A well-rounded education was important to both Anne Sullivan and Helen Keller.

Helen Keller studied very hard and, with Sullivan's help, she was accepted into Radcliffe College. This was what she had dreamt of: *"Before me I saw a new world opening in beauty and light, and I felt within me the* **capacity** *to know all things. In the wonderland of Mind I should be as free as another."* Keller felt that education made her the equal of all whose ears could hear and eyes could see.

College life wasn't easy. Keller especially struggled with math signs, and the school was very careful to make sure Sullivan wasn't helping her. But she was happy: *"Knowledge is happiness, because to have knowledge—broad, deep knowledge—is to know true ends from false, and lofty things from low."* Keller graduated, with honors, from Radcliffe in 1904.

BRAILLE

Some of Helen Keller's schoolbooks were available in Braille. Braille is a writing system that uses raised dots arranged in patterns so that people can read using their sense of touch. Louis Braille, its inventor, lost his eyesight at the age of 3. He created his writing method, still used today, when he was a teenager. By age 10, Helen had learned to read and write Braille. She would also learn to use regular and Braille typewriters, too.

Many of Helen Keller's schoolbooks would have looked like this.

This is a photo of
Helen Keller at her
graduation from Radcliffe.

BOOK *Lover*

MORE TO KNOW

Besides books, Keller was passionate about dogs. She felt that they understood her limitations and always stood close by when she was alone.

Throughout Keller's life, with the help of Braille, she maintained a strong love of books. She got top grades in English in school and never stopped reading for pleasure. After reading the *Iliad*, the famous ancient Greek poem, she declared: *"My physical limitations are forgotten—my world lies upward, the length and the breadth and the sweep of the heavens are mine!"*

Keller described books as her friends. In her opinion, books never **discriminate** based on disability or handicap. Books, and the stories within them, accepted her without hesitation and allowed her to see people and places as she never had before: *"No barrier of the senses shuts me out from the sweet, gracious **discourse** of my book-friends."*

Helen Keller is pictured with two of her favorite things: a book and a canine companion.

ALWAYS READING

Helen Keller always felt a great love for fairy tales. However, Anne Sullivan challenged her at a young age to read the classics and not just children's literature. By the age of 8, she was reading serious poems and the Bible. One of Helen Keller's favorite authors was William Shakespeare: *"I do not remember a time since I have been capable of loving books that I have not loved Shakespeare."*

WRITING

FINDING HER VOICE

While Helen Keller always had a gift for writing, she spent her life trying to perfect her speech. *"The impulse to utter **audible** sounds had always been strong within me. I used to make noises, keeping one hand on my throat while the other hand felt the movement of my lips."* She put her hands on Sullivan's mouth and throat and copied the movement and vibration. Yet, without being able to hear her own voice, she couldn't be sure how she sounded.

In 1903, while still at Radcliffe, Helen Keller published her autobiography, *The Story of My Life*. The book opened: *"It is with a kind of fear that I begin to write the history of my life."* Keller found it difficult to distinguish *"fact from fancy"* in her early years. Instead of including every detail, she said, *"I shall try to present in a series of sketches only the episodes that seem to me to be the most interesting and important."*

The World I Live In, another book she published in 1908, aimed to help others

understand what it's like living without sight and hearing. Keller described how she used her senses of smell and touch as well as her imagination to navigate the world. People were fascinated by both these extraordinary accounts.

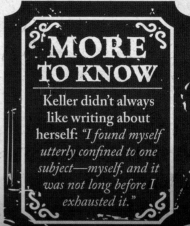

Keller's sense of smell was so well developed that she could tell one kind of rose from another.

LECTURE
Tour

Other people found Keller's story fascinating and wanted to know more about this young woman. So, Helen Keller and Anne Sullivan became famous lecturers. Describing her first talk in 1913, Keller wrote, *"Terror invaded my flesh, my mind froze, my heart stopped beating."* She ran off the stage crying! However, she tried again, beginning a 50-year career.

With each tour stop, Sullivan spoke about her years with Keller, and then Keller spoke. It was difficult for most people to understand Keller, so Sullivan repeated her words. At the end of the talk, they took questions from the audience. Their tour brought fame and an offer to have Keller's life turned into a black-and-white film called *Deliverance*. Produced in 1919, Helen Keller and Anne Sullivan appeared in it.

WOMEN'S RIGHTS

Helen Keller's lectures were an opportunity to be an **advocate** for the rights and fair treatment of the deaf, mute, and blind. She also participated in efforts to promote women's rights, especially the right to vote, which women didn't yet have. They would receive that right in 1920 with the Nineteenth Amendment. Interestingly, Anne Sullivan didn't share her views about this. In fact, she and Keller often disagreed on social issues. However, they agreed in *"our desire of good"* for the world, Keller recalled.

Anne Sullivan watches Helen Keller touch a sculpture of an eagle during their lecture tour in 1913.

AMERICAN
Foundation for the Blind

In 1924, the American Foundation for the Blind (AFB) asked Keller to become their spokesperson. *"When the public adopts an attitude of understanding and helpfulness, the difficulties of the sightless will no longer be insurmountable. Through you they will triumph over blindness,"* she said to one audience. In one night of lecturing, she raised $21,000 for the AFB, a huge sum at that time.

In 1925, Keller spoke at a major meeting of Lions Clubs, which are community service organizations. She motivated the creation of the "Knights of the Blind": *"You who have your sight, your hearing, you who are strong and brave and kind—will you not constitute yourselves Knights of the Blind* in my **crusade** *against darkness?*" This speech led to the Lions Clubs adopting vision loss as its focus for community service.

MORE TO KNOW

Helen Keller had a lifelong friendship with Alexander Graham Bell, the inventor of the telephone, who also made devices to help the deaf.

President Calvin Coolidge also did work for the American Foundation for the Blind. Coolidge and Keller are shown together here.

"WITHOUT *Teacher*"

MORE TO KNOW

Keller later said, *"I have never really felt that Teacher and I were really apart."* She believed her friend somehow lived on.

By 1936, Anne Sullivan's health was growing worse, and she finally died on October 20. She never took much credit for her role in Keller's success. She saw herself as a teacher. In a statement before she died, Sullivan said: *"Thank God I gave of my life that Helen might live."*

Shortly after her death, Keller and Polly Thomson traveled to Scotland. On the trip, Keller wrote, *"This is the first voyage Polly and I have had without Teacher, who was the life and the center of our journeyings by land and sea. . . . The anguish which makes me feel cut in two prevents me from writing another word about these life-wrecking changes."* She'd miss her friend but chose to focus on her ongoing work.

USA
15c

HELEN KELLER
ANNE SULLIVAN

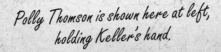
Polly Thomson is shown here at left, holding Keller's hand.

A TRIP TO JAPAN

Despite losing Sullivan, Keller continued with her mission to help the disabled worldwide. In 1937, for example, she traveled to Japan, touring 39 cities and delivering 97 lectures. Keller was extremely popular in Japan. One newspaper there reported, *"No foreign visitor had ever been accorded such an enthusiastic reception."* On that trip, she received the gift of an Akita dog, the first of its kind to be brought back to the United States.

EDUCATION
for All

WORLD WAR II

Keller was famously against war: *"What a price to pay . . . the lives of millions of young men; other millions crippled and blinded for life; existence made hideous for still more millions of human beings."* However, after World War II (1939–1945), Keller focused on bringing her experiences to men and women who had been handicapped by the conflict. She visited many military hospitals around the world. She said that visiting the soldiers who fought selflessly was *"the crowning experience"* of her life.

In the 1940s and 1950s, Helen Keller helped found schools for blind and deaf children in Africa, Asia, and Latin America. She wanted others to have the same opportunities she had. She recalled, *"I was like [a] ship before my education began, only I was without compass . . . and [I had] no way of knowing how near the harbor was. 'Light! Give me light!' was the wordless cry of my soul."* Without Anne Sullivan and the schools she attended, she never would have experienced that light.

Keller also appealed to employers to hire the blind and deaf, and even advocated for blind sports such as bowling and golf as well as Braille cookbooks. She was for anything that would allow those with disabilities to live a normal life.

Keller reads to blind children in England.

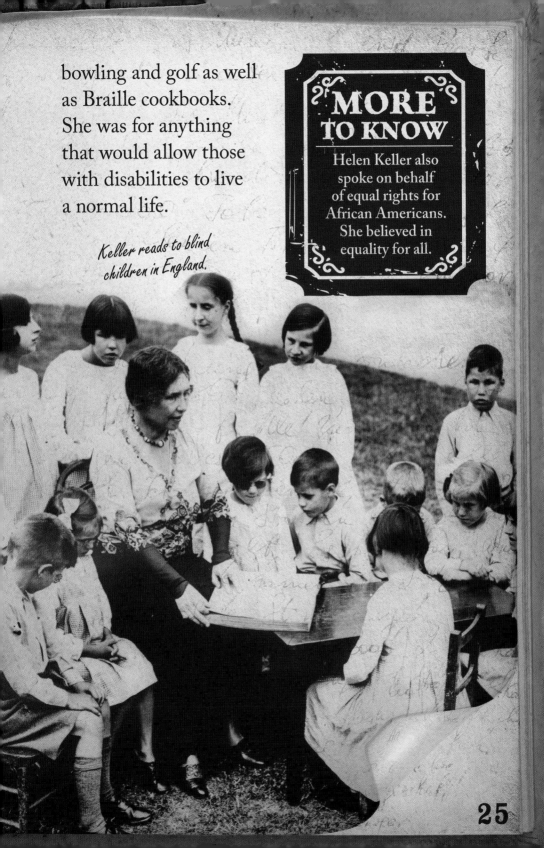

The PRESIDENTIAL
Medal of Freedom

Keller's companion Polly Thomson died in 1961. *"It will be most lonely for me,"* Keller wrote to a friend. However, she never felt too sorry for herself: *"Self-pity is our worst enemy and if we yield to it, we can never do anything good in the world."*

At 80 years old, she decided to give up traveling. She lived in a house in Connecticut where she had special rails built so that she could walk through her garden and feel the plants.

In 1964, President Lyndon B. Johnson awarded Helen Keller the Presidential Medal of Freedom, the highest honor awarded to a citizen who isn't a soldier. Sadly, she was too ill to accept the award in person by that point. She had suffered a series of strokes.

MORE TO KNOW

Keller received honorary doctoral degrees from Harvard University (the first woman to do so) and the Universities of Glasgow, Berlin, Delhi, and Johannesburg.

Helen Keller maintained a great love for nature throughout her life. →

THE MIRACLE WORKER

Author Mark Twain once called Anne Sullivan a *"miracle worker"* for how she transformed Keller's life. In 1957, William Gibson wrote a play called *The Miracle Worker*. He used parts of Keller's autobiography *The Story of My Life* in the play to describe key events in the lives of the two remarkable women. The play won several awards and is still performed today in many places. It became a movie in 1962.

DEATH
and Legacy

MORE TO KNOW

In 1988, the Helen Keller Foundation for Research and Education was founded by Keller's family.

Helen Keller died on June 1, 1968, only a few weeks before her eighty-eighth birthday. Her ashes were placed with Anne Sullivan's and Polly Thomson's at the National Cathedral in Washington, DC.

Keller once said, *"Character cannot be developed in ease and quiet. Only through experience of trial and suffering can the soul be strengthened, ambition inspired, and success achieved."* Since the first day Keller began to learn to communicate with the world, she was a continuous example of these words and the extraordinary success one can accomplish with perseverance.

The woman who devoted so much of her life to others may have passed away, but her ultimate triumph over her disabilities still encourages others to achieve their dreams.

Helen Keller was such an important public figure that her image was featured on a US quarter.

TIMELINE
THE LIFE OF HELEN KELLER

1880 — Helen Keller is born June 27 in Tuscumbia, Alabama

1882 — Keller develops a fever that leaves her blind and deaf

1887 — Anne Sullivan arrives in Tuscumbia

1888 — Keller enters Perkins School for the Blind

1890 — Keller begins Horace Mann School for the Deaf

1894 — Keller attends Wright-Humason School for the Deaf

1896 — Keller enters Cambridge School

1903 — Keller publishes *The Story of My Life*

1904 — Keller graduates with honors from Radcliffe

1913 — Keller and Sullivan give their first lecture

1924 — American Foundation for the Blind (AFB) asks Keller to become spokesperson

1936 — Sullivan dies on October 20

1937 — Keller visits Japan

1946 — Keller begins worldwide tour of military hospitals and promotes establishment of schools for disabled

1964 — President Lyndon B. Johnson awards Keller Presidential Medal of Freedom

1968 — Helen Keller dies June 1

A LIFE OF SERVICE, ADMIRED

At a memorial service for Helen Keller in Washington, DC, Senator Lister Hill of Keller's home state of Alabama recalled that Keller *"employed the symbol of her own courage and faith to the benefit of millions of her fellow handicapped in America and throughout the world."* This is why *"Wherever she went, she was received with a massive outpouring of love and admiration; she was honored by heads of state; she was acclaimed by all."*

GLOSSARY

abstract: a thought or idea that isn't connected to a physical object

acute congestion: a condition that causes severe swelling

advocate: one who supports or speaks in favor of something

anguish: strong pain or suffering

audible: loud or clear enough to be heard

autobiography: a book written by someone about their life

capacity: the ability to do or experience something

crusade: an action to promote a cause

discourse: a discussion about something between people

discriminate: to unfairly treat people unequally

impel: to make someone feel the need to do something

insurmountable: describing something that cannot be overcome

persevere: to persist steadily in action or belief, usually over a long period and despite problems

FOR MORE
Information

Books

Garrett, Leslie. *Helen Keller*. New York, NY: DK Publishing, 2013.

Hollingsworth, Tamara Leigh. *Helen Keller: A New Vision*. Huntington Beach, CA: Teacher Created Materials, 2013.

Peck, Audrey. *Helen Keller: Miracle Child*. New York, NY: PowerKids Press, 2013.

Websites

Helen Keller Biography
www.afb.org/info/about-us/helen-keller/biography-and-chronology/biography/1235
Read the American Foundation for the Blind's biography of Helen Keller.

Helen Keller Foundation for Research and Education
www.helenkellerfoundation.org/home.asp
Find out what the Helen Keller Foundation for Research and Education is doing to battle blindness and deafness.

INDEX